OCT 2012

FREAKING OUT!

The Science of the Teenage Brain

By Dana Meachen Rau

COMPASS POINT BOOKS
a capstone imprint

Compass Point Books
1710 Roe Crest Drive
North Mankato, MN 56003

Editors: Sarah Eason and Geoff Barker
Designers: Paul Myerscough and Geoff Ward
Media Researcher: Susannah Jayes
Content Consultant: Harold Pratt, President, Educational Consultants Inc.
and Science Curriculum Inc.
Production Specialist: Laura Manthe

With special thanks to William H. Church, Associate Professor of Chemistry and
Neuroscience, Trinity College, Hartford, Connecticut, for reviewing this manuscript,
and to Sam Flower, Jay Cizeski, and Katrina Zawasky for sharing their stories.

Image Credits

Alamy: Catchlight Visual Services 42b, Nick Gregory 20b; Corbis: Blend Images/Sam Bloomberg-Rissman 23,
Sygma/John Van Hasselt 16b, David Turnley 10–11, Holger Winkler 6ml; Geoff Ward: 6b, 13t; **Getty Images:**
Jordan Strauss/WireImage 26b; **Photo Researchers, Inc:** US National Library of Medicine 9; **Shutterstock:**
3dimentil 39 (balls), 4designersart 12bl, absolute-india back cover, 30t, 32t, 34t, 36l, Andresr 3, 8b,
Apollofoto 21, Yuri Arcurs 46t, AVAVA 58r, Betacam-SP 5, bikeriderlondon 57, blue67design cover (doodles),
Brian Chase 37, Lars Christensen 36r, CREATISTA 1, 43, 45, Dhoxax 40–41, Flashon Studio 50–51, Mike Flippo
4b, foto.fritz 35b, Biaj Gabriel 55r, Gelpi 15, 24b, Jose Gil 19bg, 27 t, 40m, 56m, 59tr, Sean Gladwell 17t,
hartphotography 39 (kids), Jomphong 30b, Lana K 46–47, Gongul Kokal 59b, Max Krasnov 44l, Kruglov_Orda
48–49, Layland Masuda 4 t, 6 t, 8 t, 10 t, Dean Mitchell 63, Monkey Business Images 27 b, 53, Oksana2010
28, Olly 19, OtnaYdur 61, Daniel Padavona 17b, Ioannis Pantziaras 12t, 14t, 16t, 18t, Catalin Petolea 38t,
40t, 42t, 44t, James M. Phelps Jr. 56b, photomak 48l, 52, Glenda M Powers 32–33, Primusold 35t, Bruce Roiff
60b, Pete Saloutos 12–13b, 55l, Henri Schmit 59tl, Andrey Shadrin 54tl, 56tl, 58tl, 60t, Ljupco Smokovski
14b, Jason Stitt 44r, Lorraine Swanson 31, tatniz 6–7, Gladskikh Tatiana 26m, Todd Taulman 22, Benjamin
Thorn 25, Pedro Vidal 7r, VikaSuh 38b, Vlue 20t, 24t, 26t, 32m, 51t, Tony Wear, cover (boy), Julian Weber
cover (design element), Tracy Whiteside 18b.

Library of Congress Cataloging-in-Publication Data
Rau, Dana Meachen, 1971–
    Freaking out! : the science of the teenage brain / by Dana Meachen Rau.
        p. cm.—(Everyday science)
    Includes bibliographical references and index.
    ISBN 978-0-7565-4486-7 (library binding)
    ISBN 978-0-7565-4500-0 (paperback)
    1. Brain—Juvenile literature. 2. Brain—Physiology—Juvenile literature. I. Title.
    QP376.R37 2012
    612.8—dc22   2010054302

Visit Compass Point Books on the Internet at *www.capstonepub.com*

Printed in the United States of America in North Mankato, Minnesota.
062012
006767R

table of contents

who's the boss?

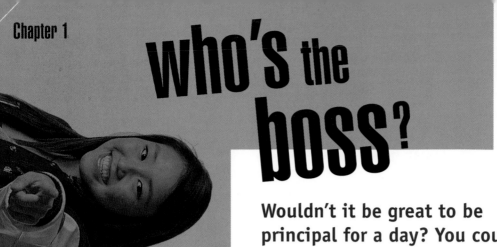

Wouldn't it be great to be principal for a day? You could put your feet up on a desk, boss around the teachers, and make all the decisions for your school. Maybe you'd cancel all classes and have a party on the soccer field.

Although all brains are made up of the same parts, each person's brain gives them an individual personality.

Your brain is like a principal—it's the boss of your body. It powers your muscles. It tells your heart to beat, throat to swallow, and eyes to blink. It tells you when to sleep—even if you're sitting in the middle of social studies class.

But your brain's not just a motor making your separate parts run. It also does all the thinking. Your brain decides if you want chips or cookies from the vending machine. It remembers, or sometimes forgets, your locker combination. Your brain houses your emotions—such as embarrassment when your binder drops and spews paper all over the hallway. Most importantly, your brain makes you ... YOU. All of your fellow students have basically the same parts as you. But wouldn't it be creepy if everyone acted the same? Your brains give each one of you a unique personality.

Your brain might be what gives you your sparkling, awesome, or magnetic personality, but it's not very attractive on its own. The brain's a lump of gray, bumpy, squishy tissue that weighs about 3 pounds (1.4 kilograms). It doesn't look like much. But there's a lot of powerful stuff going on in there.

FACT!

Brain Maps

One way scientists study brains is with an fMRI (functional Magnetic Resonance Imaging) machine. This equipment takes images of brain activity. Scientists can watch which areas of the brain are more active while the person performs certain tasks.

Brain Matters

The three main parts of the brain, from top to bottom, are cerebrum, cerebellum, and brain stem. The cerebrum looks like a tangle of ridges and bumps. The outer layer of the cerebrum is the cortex.

Think of a napkin. If you laid it out flat, it would cover a pretty big area. But if you crumple it up, it can fit in your pocket. Your cortex is crumpled for the same reason. It has a large surface area, but it is compressed into a smaller space so it can fit in your head.

Logic on the left

The left side of your brain is the nerve center for your scientific and logical thoughts.

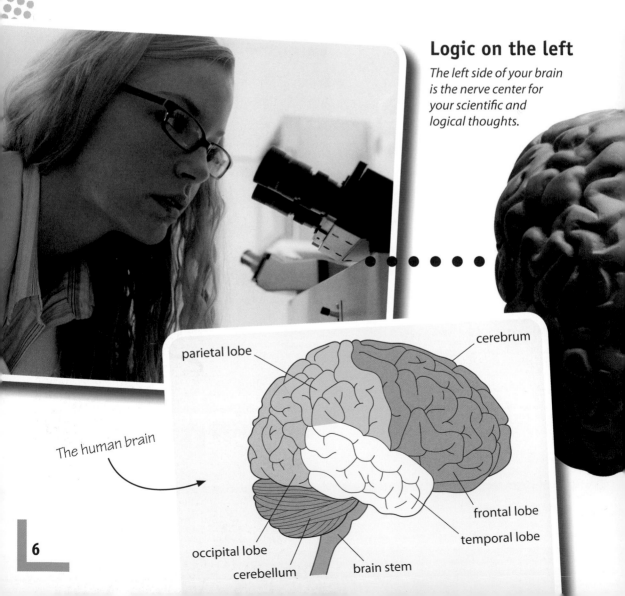

The human brain

parietal lobe

cerebrum

frontal lobe

temporal lobe

occipital lobe

cerebellum

brain stem

Groovy Stuff

Besides all of the bumps and valleys, the cerebrum has a deep groove down the center. This line divides the brain into the right hemisphere and the left hemisphere. Each of the hemispheres is made up of four areas called lobes. A bridge of nerves called the corpus callosum connects both hemispheres so they can communicate with each other.

Right, Left, Right, Left

The right and left hemispheres of your brain have different functions, although they work together on most tasks. The left deals with logical thoughts; the right is more creative. The left hemisphere controls the motor functions of the right side of your body, and the right hemisphere controls the left side.

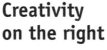

Creativity on the right

Music, art, photography—the right side of your brain is a creative powerhouse.

Hard Worker

Your cerebrum probably has the most work to do. It holds your thoughts, memories, and all the things you've ever learned. It determines your personality and how you relate to other people. It takes in information from your senses, decodes what it means, and decides what to do next.

The cerebrum is the largest area of your brain. This part allows you to read, write, speak, and make decisions.

Do the wrong thing?

Do the right thing?

The Man with a Hole in His Head

Back in 1848 Phineas Gage was setting explosives for the construction of a railroad track in Vermont. In the explosion his 3-foot (1-meter) tamping rod shot like a bullet up from the ground. It flew into his cheek, through the front of his brain and skull, and out of his forehead.

Phineas survived. In fact, he could walk, talk, eat, and function as he had before the accident. But Phineas was different. Before the accident he had been a reliable worker. After it he had trouble getting along with others. His personality completely changed. Many doctors studied, and still study, Phineas' case. Since the iron rod had damaged Phineas' frontal lobe, doctors were able to learn what role this area of the brain plays in brain function.

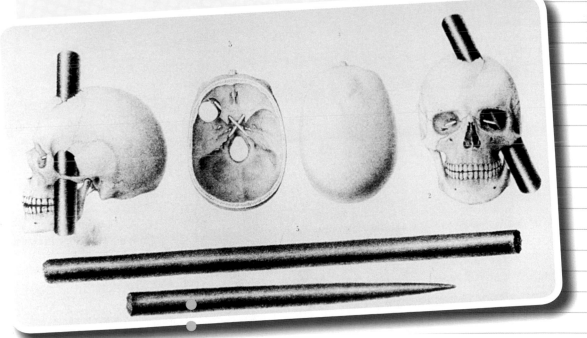

If an object enters the frontal lobe of the brain, the damage caused can change someone's personality beyond recognition.

Balancing Act

The cerebellum is tucked up under the cerebrum. It's the go-to guy for keeping you balanced. The brain stem takes information from all parts of your body and keeps your body working properly. It also takes care of the things you don't usually have to think about—such as regulating your heart rate, breathing, and body temperature.

A principal is no good to anyone if she just locks herself in her office all day. A good principal listens to her students. In return, the students listen to their principal. Your brain listens to your body, and in return, your body obeys the brain's commands.

"AHA!" Moments

Have you ever tried to solve a puzzle when "AHA!" you suddenly know the answer? Using fMRIs, scientists have studied which parts of the brain turn on immediately before an "AHA!" moment.

Try this puzzle:

Joe is not a superhero. He's not a magician. He's not a ghost. He is just a regular kid. But he can walk through walls. How can he do this?

You may find when you focus a lot of energy analyzing and laboring over a solution, you can't get it. But when you take a step back, your brain is able to search and explore for other possible answers.

No matter how long it took to solve the puzzle above, the answer seems obvious once you get it. The answer? He can walk through a door.

Essential for gymnastics, the cerebellum provides precise timing for coordinated muscle movements.

11

running a relay

Your spinal cord is the large collection of nerves leading out of your brain and down through a canal in your spinal column. It's like the main hallway through your school. More nerves lead off the spinal cord, winding their way around your body to every organ, every finger and toe, every spot on your skin.

FACT!

Losing the Connection

When someone's spinal cord is damaged, the motor neurons that normally bring messages to the brain may be destroyed. The person might suffer paralysis and no longer be able to move his or her arms or legs.

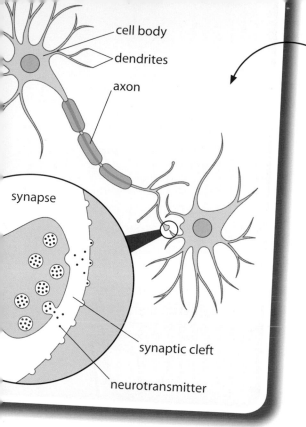

cell body

dendrites

axon

synapse

synaptic cleft

neurotransmitter

Message delivered

Take a Closer Look

Zoom in even closer, and you can see an individual nerve cell. Also known as a neuron, a nerve cell is made up of a main cell body with branches coming off it. Dendrites are the branches on one end that take in information. On the other end, there's a longer fiber called an axon. The axon passes the information along to the next neuron.

Neurons work like members of a relay team. To get to the finish line, a relay team needs each member to perform in proper sequence, passing the baton from one runner to the next. A neuron takes in information through its dendrites. The information becomes an electrical impulse—maybe that's why the symbol for a great idea is a light bulb. The information travels through the cell to its axon, down the axon to the terminal. Then it is passed on to the next neuron's dendrites. Information is processed by neurons passing impulses from one to the next, traveling through your brain and body.

Imagine the connections between nerve cells in the body as hands exchanging the baton in a mega-fast relay race.

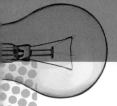
Bridging the Gap

Neurons do not actually touch each other. The point where the information is transferred from one neuron to the next is called the synapse. There are three parts to the synapse—the neuron sending the information, the space between the neurons known as the synaptic cleft, and the neuron receiving the information. The impulse from the sending neuron can't leap across the space to the receiving neuron, so a special messenger is recruited to carry the information across the gap. This special messenger is a chemical called a neurotransmitter. The sending cell tells the neurotransmitter to float across the synaptic cleft to the receiving neuron.

Here comes the messenger!

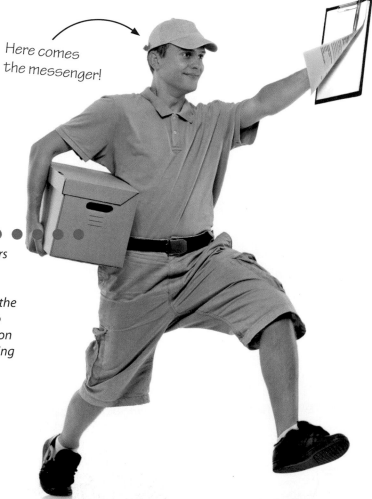

Neurotransmitters are the body's couriers, leaping over any gaps in the message route to deliver information to waiting receiving neurons.

Let the Rumors Fly!

Have you ever confided a secret in a friend only to have the information come back to you days later completely incorrect? That's how rumors spread, because information changes or gets exaggerated as it passes from person to person.

Try this classic game of telephone to see how your message changes as it's passed along.

You will need:
- A large group of people (the more the merrier)

1. Stand or sit in a circle. Whisper a sentence to the person on your right. Make sure it's not too short and try to make it a little odd, like "potato chips go great with grape soda, especially if you eat them under an umbrella." Or "Claire keeps a Superman cape in her backpack in case the front desk secretary tells her to fetch a coffee."

2. The next person whispers the message to the person on the right, and so on until the message comes back to you.

3. Did you receive the same message you sent? If it's not the same, try to figure out where the message went wrong. Luckily, your neurons are a lot better at passing along messages!

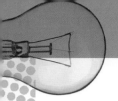

Sensing the World

How do your nerves and your brain, locked up inside your body, know what's going on outside it? That's where your senses come in. The five senses—sight, hearing, smell, touch, and taste—are your brain's windows to the world. Special sensory neurons take in the information—hot sauce on your tongue, a friend poking you from behind, the crash of a book hitting the floor—and send the news along to other neurons until the message reaches the brain. Then it's the boss's job to process that information and tell the appropriate parts of your body what to do.

Hoagie Wednesday in the Cafeteria

You snag a tray, a carton of milk, and a full plate. Your eyes see the packed sandwich, bursting with meat and cheese, cradled in golden brown bread. Mmmm... Your nose smells the spicy mustard. You remember how delicious it was last week. Your stomach growls in agreement. Your brain has processed these sights and smells, combined it with memories, and made your body react.

If you lose one of your senses your brain then focuses on the remaining senses. Some gifted musicians, such as the late Ray Charles, are blind, but have excellent hearing.

Ouch!

Not all senses are pleasant. Have you ever slammed your locker shut with your thumb still inside? The sensory neurons in your thumb rush the information to your brain to tell it you're hurt. Pain actually protects you. Without pain, you might bump into things all day and you wouldn't know you were hurting your body.

If you've ever taken a hit during a football game, you'll know that it really hurts. The pain is a message from your brain telling you "this feels wrong—move out of the way!"

Hey, That Hurt!

Why does the doctor hit your knee with a hammer? She does it to check your reflexes. Your body has a lot of involuntary reflexes that you don't do on purpose—like when your pupils expand to let in more light, or when you sneeze to get rid of dust in your nose. A stimulus (such as the hammer hitting your knee, the lack of light, or the dust) starts the reflex. Then the information is sent to your central nervous system. Instead of the brain processing the information, the spinal cord takes in the message and tells the motor nerves how to act. So when the doctor hits you with a hammer, she doesn't mean to hurt you. She's making sure your reflexes work as they should.

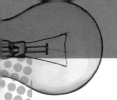

Move Along

Your brain also sends messages along neurons to tell your body how to move. Motor neurons communicate with the muscles all over your body—the muscles in your arms and legs, your torso, and even the many muscles just in your face.

The language centers of your brain tell your lips, tongue, and vocal cords how to move to form words.

The brain is more than just the headquarters that takes in messages and gives out commands. It can also talk to itself. Call it crazy if you want, but that's how thinking works.

Let them have it, motor neurons!

● *Even arguing with your friends requires*
● *motor neurons—they control the muscles in*
● *your face to create those really crazy, angry*
● *expressions that tell people just how you feel.*

true tales

Quick Thinking Saves a Life

At summer camp Jay and his friends were heading down the trail to the mess hall for lunch. One of the kids tripped, fell, and hit his head on a rock. Jay took off for the infirmary to find the nurse. She was more than half a mile away. "I had never run that fast in my life," he says. Luckily, the boy was brought to the hospital and everything turned out OK, even though he had lost a lot of blood. "If I hadn't had that quick burst of energy,"

Jay remembers, "the situation would have been a lot worse."

How did Jay get a sudden burst of energy? His frontal cortex quickly assessed the situation and made a decision—to run for help. The frontal cortex sent a message to his hypothalamus at the top of the brain stem. The message continued to his pituitary (just below the hypothalamus), then down his body to his adrenal glands (on top of the kidneys). These glands released the chemical epinephrine into his bloodstream, giving him the speed he needed to get help in time.

Have you ever run faster than you ever thought you could? It might have been epinephrine pumping into your body to give you the speed you needed.

what were you thinking?!

If you have an easy worksheet for homework, you might call it a "no-brainer." It's so easy you don't even need to use your brain. But you do use it—for everything.

The brain itself is made of neurons. Not only are there trillions of neurons in your brain, but each neuron makes connections with lots of other neurons, resulting in more than 60 trillion synapses. That's a lot of possible paths for impulses to travel. Your cortex, also called gray matter because of its color, does most of the thinking. As you grow, your gray matter thickens with many layers of neurons. More neurons mean the potential for more connections between them.

Don't give up!

● ● ● ● ● ● ● ● ●

The brain processes lots of information at the same time. It helps you coordinate the fingers of both hands when you play the guitar.

Use It or Lose It

Some pathways, such as the hallways in your school or the sidewalk around it, are well defined. They're used so much that they have become permanent ways to get from place to place. You can make a new path across the grass to the baseball field. And if you walked that same route every day, the grass would get trampled. The more you travel it, the clearer the path will become. This is like what happens in your brain.

Some scientists call this the "use it or lose it" principle. If you use a pathway a lot—such as playing the guitar every day or practicing your pitching skills—it will become clearer. If you don't use a pathway very much, it will dry up.

Remember—practice makes perfect! If you have a skill, you will still need to practice.

Multitasking: Getting More Done, or Nothing Done Well?

When it's time to do homework, do you shut out all distractions, sit at a quiet desk, and concentrate? It's more likely that you have some distractions—maybe the dog's barking, your brother's on the phone, and your sister's watching a TV show. Life is busy and it's sometimes impossible to shut out all distractions. People like to think they can multitask—do more than one thing at a time. But is it possible? Try this experiment to find out.

You will need:
- A deck of cards
- A television
- A timer or watch

1. Turn on a TV show you really enjoy to an episode you haven't seen before (in other words, you really want to see it).
2. Drop the deck of cards onto the floor so it falls into a messy pile.
3. Your job is to put the cards back into a deck organized by suit and in order within each suit (from ace to king).

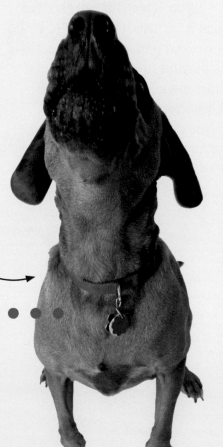

Be quiet!

The sound of a barking dog can be enough to drive you crazy—and make working impossible.

4. Start the timer or note the time and sort the cards. Write down your time when you're done. How long did it take?

5. Now turn off the TV. Drop the cards and sort them again. How long did it take this time?

Think about how this applies to doing homework. Wouldn't you rather be done with your homework faster? Fewer distractions can make that happen, because you're not asking your brain to process two streams of information at once.

Keeping up with your friends is fun, but wait until you've finished your homework.

Your Growing Brain

You're not born with all the brain cells you'll have for the rest of your life. Your brain develops the most during two critical times—when you're a baby and when you're a teenager. When you're a baby, your brain creates and organizes its pathways as you learn how to move, how to talk, and what words mean. When you're a teenager, your brain forges new pathways—mostly related to making decisions and seeking pleasure.

Think of all the movements, thoughts, and feelings the brain of a baby or toddler has to process when doing seemingly simple tasks, such as learning to walk.

Here goes ...

The Right Decision?

The frontal cortex is where your brain processes information to help you make decisions, make friends, and make plans. In teenagers, however, your frontal cortex is not yet fully developed. Your brain is still growing new neurons and refining pathways.

So when you're making decisions, you're bound to make some mistakes. Maybe you decide to invite the new girl to your birthday party. You find out really fast (when she starts bullying your best friend) that it was a bad idea. Maybe you decide to eat an early dinner at a friend's house. But when you come home, your mom made your favorite pasta and you're too full to enjoy it. If your parents ask, "What were you thinking?," you can blame it on your brain.

The good news is that your cortex has some backup to help it make good decisions. The corpus callosum helps you solve problems.

The cerebellum not only balances your body so it doesn't fall over, but it also helps balance your thought processes. The parts of your brain are connected by a whole network of neurons that pull together needed information. Your brain will retrieve past, similar experiences to make a better decision the next time. In other words, you can learn from your own mistakes.

Shall I go swimming? Or should I do my homework first? Gradually we learn to make better decisions.

FACT!

Growing Up Fast

*You're so immature!
Don't be offended.
If you're a teenager, your brain isn't fully
developed yet. That's normal. Brains
aren't fully mature until about age 25.*

*But you're lucky too. Since your brain
is still growing, it's actively making
connections between neurons. As you
get older, connections start to break
down. By the time you're an old man
or woman, your brain has lost a lot of
brain cells and even shrinks.*

Developing Skills

Your brain takes in information—
the good and the bad—and uses it
to decide which pathways to make
permanent and which ones to leave
behind. If you spend all of your
time "talking" to friends by texting
or on the computer, you may not
develop the same skills you would
get by face-to-face relationships.
On the flip side, if you spend time
honing a skill—such as cooking,
sports, art, skateboarding, or any
other passion you wish to follow—
you'll likely have that skill well
into your adult life.

*Superstar legends
such as Tony
Hawk practiced
and practiced
their boarding
skills until they
were perfect. Do
the same, and one
day you might be
a skateboarding
superstar.*

26

true tales

How Smart Is That?

Bill Gates was only 15 when he started making money from the computer programs he created. Now he's a billionaire. There's no doubt Bill Gates is a smart man. But what does being smart really mean? There's no one test that can measure your intelligence—how well your brain can learn new knowledge and use that knowledge again. Intelligence is your ability to understand, analyze, and make decisions. Intelligence is how well you interact with others, face problems, and find solutions. In other words, intelligence is how well your brain works. The grades on your report card only show a tiny bit of how "smart" you are.

Texting friends involves complex eye-hand coordination, reading, and emotions, but try to still work on your face-to-face relationships.

Testing the Stroop Effect

J. Ridley Stroop published an article in a psychology journal in the 1930s. In his study he tested subjects on how fast they could read color words—such as red, blue, and green. However, the words were printed in inks that were not the same color as the words themselves.
Try recreating his experiment here.

1. Time yourself naming the colors of each of the words in list one.
2. Time yourself reading the colors of the words in list two. Remember, you're not reading the words themselves. You need to name the color of the word.
3. How do your times compare?

You will need:
- Two lists of color words (right)
- A timer or watch

● *Ready, set, go!*

LIST ONE

Red	Brown	Red	Yellow
Green	Pink	Purple	Orange
Orange	Black	Pink	Blue
Purple	Green	Brown	Green
Yellow	Blue	Black	Purple

LIST TWO

Orange	Blue	Brown	Red
Brown	Green	Pink	Green
Black	Purple	Black	Blue
Yellow	Pink	Green	Purple
Orange	Yellow	Blue	Pink

Did it take you longer to read the second list?
That's because your brain is getting competing bits
of information—the word doesn't match the color.
So it takes it a little more time to sort out the answer.

just forget it

Imagine this. You're headed to your science lab for a big test. A bunch of facts are swimming around in your head. There is so much to remember!

But the test answers aren't all you need to remember to get yourself to class and take the test. You have to remember what hallway your class is in. You have to remember how to open a door, cross the room, and sit in your chair. You have to remember how to use a pencil ... that is, if you remembered to bring one.

Live and Learn

Memory plays a huge part in your everyday life. When you take in information about the world, you're learning about it. You store what you've learned in your brain. But your memory's not like a binder with labeled and organized information. You can't just flip through memories neatly recorded on sheets of loose-leaf paper. Many parts of the brain play a role in each memory.

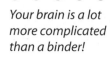

Your brain is a lot more complicated than a binder!

Maybe it's the first day of school, and you have a new homeroom teacher. You walk into class and instantly recognize her. She's the woman from the deli line at the grocery store who accused you of cutting in front of her. You clearly remember the whole event—how you didn't realize she was there when you stepped up to the counter. How you blushed when she scolded you. How you just wanted the deli guy to hand over the bologna so you could get out of the store.

Every time you make your way through the school corridor to your locker, you are using your memory.

FACT!

Amnesia

You may have read a story or seen a show about a character with amnesia—some poor guy wakes up one morning not knowing who he is or where he came from. Amnesia is a real condition when a patient loses significant amounts of memory. It's as if someone highlighted all of someone's memories and then hit a delete button. Through therapy, hypnosis, or drugs, doctors can help patients recall their lost memories.

Amnesia is caused by a head injury, a stroke, or a traumatic event. The frontal cortex and the hippocampus, which is in charge of transferring memories from short term to long term, lose their connection. The pathways for recalling memories can't be accessed any more.

Our brains keep some information and filter out the rest. You might not remember anything else about your class party except for whacking the piñata.

Working Together

Various centers in the brain deal with senses, emotions, and learned actions. So they all work together when you recall a memory. The hippocampus in the brain pulls bits of separate information together to form a complete memory. Sometimes the pathways between parts of the brain for a specific memory are well traveled. This is true for a memory you recall often, wrote about in a diary, or have pictures to help you remember it well.

When your brain pulls together separate bits from an episode in your past, it is rebuilding the event. Some parts of the whole experience may actually be missing. Maybe you had a really strict third-grade teacher who gave you lots of homework every night. But that's not what you remember from that particular year. Instead you remember the bang-up Valentine's Day party when she let each of you take a whack at the piñata.

Memorizing Strategies

Why is it that you can remember the name of every kid in your math class, but you can't remember all the kinds of triangles? You use the names of your classmates every day. By repeating them over and over, they shift from short-term into long-term memory. If your classmates had names like equilateral, isosceles, and scalene, you'd remember them too.

But repetition isn't the only way to retain a memory. It also helps to associate the thing you are trying to remember with something you already know. For example, your locker combination may be a random collection of numbers. But if you can connect those numbers to memories you already have, you're more likely to remember them. Maybe your mom's birthday is on the 15th of the month, your house number is 22, and you have three brothers. Now 15, 22, 3 is easy to remember.

Making the Connection

Some memory experts suggest connecting seemingly random items into a strange story. Picture this. A big bag of flour throws an egg and knocks over the sugar bowl. Now you won't forget to pick up the three ingredients you need to make cookies.

You can also use an acrostic (the first letter of each word) to help you remember a list. For example, to remember the five Great Lakes, just remember the word "HOMES."

Huron
Ontario
Michigan
Erie
Superior

HOMES

Long, Short, and Really Short

Scientists generally break down memory into three types: sensory memory, short-term memory, and long-term memory. Sensory memory may only last a second. Your senses pull in information and store it in your brain. But it's quickly replaced with more information. If you pay attention to that information and give it meaning, it becomes part of your short-term memory. Short-term memory can last up to a minute. Say you're in the lunch line. As you pass through, you notice all of the choices on the counter. But by the time you get to your seat, you probably wouldn't be able to name them all.

Remember people's names better by using simple memory tricks. Repeat their name in your mind. If their surname is Hamm, imagine them carrying a huge piece of ham.

Longer Memories

If you work a little harder, you can keep information in your short-term memory for a while. If you've ever had to memorize a map, you may have repeated the names of the countries and tested yourself on them. Then you were able to keep them in your short-term memory long enough to ace the quiz. If you don't review them again after the quiz is over, they'll leave your short-term memory.

Remember the Story about the Dog ...?

If you exercise the pathways that reconstruct a memory, it becomes part of your long- term memory. Maybe every year at Thanksgiving, Uncle Fred brings up the story of the dog he found on the roof. Because he repeats it every year, no one will forget it. You may hold on to long-term memories for months, years, and even the rest of your life.

You may be sick and tired of hearing the story about the dog on the roof, but one thing is for sure, the more often you hear the story, the more you will remember it!

Memory Game

How well can you or your friends remember 10 random items? Try this simple game.

You will need:
- 10 items from around the house or classroom—the more random the selection the better—such as a paper clip, a sock, a watch, a screwdriver, a candle, etc.
- A tray
- A towel
- A friend or group of friends
- Pads and pencils

1. Collect the various items and place them on the tray.
2. Cover the tray with a towel so no one can see under it. Bring it over to the group.
3. Uncover the tray, and show your friends the items for 10 seconds. Then cover it with the towel again so the items are hidden.
4. Give your friends two minutes to write down all of the items they can remember.
5. Reveal the items. How many did they list? Which ones did they miss?
6. Ask them what tricks they used to remember the items. You may find everyone uses a different strategy.
7. Have them try again using a different strategy. Which way works best?

on the mood swing

epinephrine

Maybe you woke up today feeling grouchy. In first period you were happy to hear the book report was postponed. But in second period you got mad when a friend copied your paper. At lunch you were afraid the lunch lady would yell at you for dropping your milk. Last period you felt relief— the day was over.

serotonin

FACT!

Artificial Intelligence

Thousands of science fiction books and movies have been written about the idea of artificial intelligence—computers that can think and act as humans do. Some computers can make decisions based on past experience and adapt to their surroundings.

But the network of connections in a human brain is so complex—taking in information from so many pathways and putting them in the context of emotions, memories, and sensory experience—that it could never be recreated by artificial means.

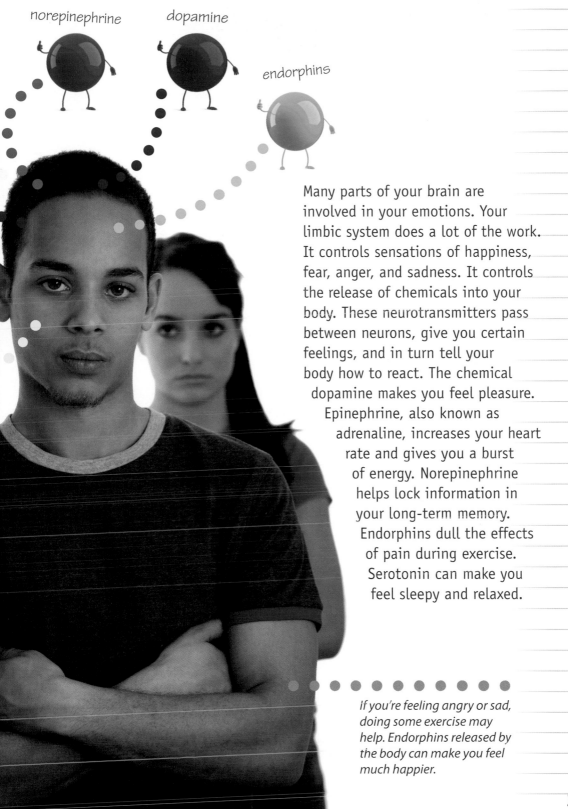

norepinephrine

dopamine

endorphins

Many parts of your brain are involved in your emotions. Your limbic system does a lot of the work. It controls sensations of happiness, fear, anger, and sadness. It controls the release of chemicals into your body. These neurotransmitters pass between neurons, give you certain feelings, and in turn tell your body how to react. The chemical dopamine makes you feel pleasure. Epinephrine, also known as adrenaline, increases your heart rate and gives you a burst of energy. Norepinephrine helps lock information in your long-term memory. Endorphins dull the effects of pain during exercise. Serotonin can make you feel sleepy and relaxed.

If you're feeling angry or sad, doing some exercise may help. Endorphins released by the body can make you feel much happier.

true tales

Fear of Dolls

Sam, an eighth-grader, is afraid of puppets, clowns, and mimes. One time Sam's sister played a practical joke on him. "My sister put a doll on my bed," Sam says. She hid a walkie talkie under the bed. "She started talking like the doll." Sam leaped out of bed in terror. Soon after, though, he realized it was a joke. "I did figure it out when the static hit," he says.

A phobia is an irrational fear. Some phobias are common, such as a fear of flying, known as aerophobia, or a fear of small spaces, known as claustrophobia.

But did you know there's a fear of the sun (heliophobia), fear of vegetables (lachanophobia), and fear of going to school (didaskaleinophobia)? You might not think these are things to be afraid of, but to a person with a phobia, fear of the object or situation makes perfect sense in his or her brain.

Sam's not alone. Many people fear clowns, dolls, or puppets because they do not act in a way that makes sense. They resemble people, yet they can stare without blinking, move strangely, and not speak. That's why horror movies and haunted houses often include clowns and dolls.

Itsy, bitsy spider climbed up the water spout ... ahhhh!

Now I'm Really Scared

Even if horror movies don't scare you, fear is a major emotion that dictates how you act. Maybe you're in the middle of gym playing dodgeball. The biggest kid in the class has been hurling balls at you all period. You see him wind up and fling his arm forward. You duck to protect yourself. Only after you're crouched and weeping on the floor do you realize he's still holding the ball. He just faked you out.

Your gut reaction was to duck, because you were afraid you'd be hit by the ball. Your "gut" isn't in your stomach. It's in your amygdala, part of your limbic system. After you ducked, you used your cortex, the thinking part of your brain, to take in more information about your surroundings—and noticed that the boy hadn't thrown the ball. You weren't in danger, but your body was protecting you just in case.

One very common phobia is called arachnophobia. If you're arachnophobic you're scared of spiders—big and small.

Good Job!

Pleasure is another important emotion that drives what you do. You crave things that make you happy—such as eating pizza, acing a test, winning a trophy, or relaxing on weekends.

Remember when you were little, and your teacher would give you a sticker for a job well done? Once you got a sticker, you would continue trying to please her so you could get another one. A sticker might not cut it any more, but your brain still likes to be rewarded. When you enjoy something, your brain releases dopamine and makes you feel good.

Your body reacts to your feelings. If you're worried, your heart beats faster. If you're afraid, your palms may sweat. Emotions are also closely tied to memory. That's why you remember happy, sad, or scary times.

Doesn't it feel great to win something? The "high" you feel is a result of the hormone dopamine, which is released by your brain.

Messing with the System

Your body naturally releases the appropriate neurotransmitter when it's needed. Medicines work because they imitate, block, or encourage the natural system of neurotransmitters. That's good if you have a headache. Taking a painkiller will block the message of pain from traveling between neurons. But drugs, such as alcohol, tobacco, and others, will trick your body into thinking things that may not be true.

For example, some drugs give you the same pleasurable feeling that dopamine does. With repeated use of these drugs, your body becomes addicted and relies on them to experience pleasure.

Drugs aren't the only thing you can become addicted to. If you enjoy video games, your body probably produces dopamine when you're playing them. The more you play, the more your body craves them to get that pleasurable dose of dopamine.

FACT!

Boys vs. Girls

Scientists have done many studies on the differences between male and female brains. Whose brain is better? It is true that on average male brains are slightly larger than female brains. But women have more tightly packed neurons, so there are more connections between them. Female brains mature earlier and have some parts, such as the frontal lobe and limbic system, which are larger than in male brains. The parietal cortex and the amygdala are larger in boys than in girls.

Anger comes from the amygdala and can have negative effects on the brain and body. The good news is that anger can quickly dissolve into laughter.

Understanding the Teenage Brain

Do you ever feel that your parents don't understand you? But did you know that's because you and your parents make decisions and plans using different parts of your brains? Adults make most decisions using their cortex. Since your cortex isn't fully developed, you make a lot of decisions using your amygdala. Imagine you have three tests tomorrow, a paper due, and your computer's not working. You might yell in frustration and decide to throw your textbook down the stairs. (Maybe not such a good idea.) Thinking more logically with your cortex can help make a monumental problem less overwhelming. When your parents say things like "It's not the end of the world" or "Put it in perspective" its not that they don't understand you. They're trying to help you react less with your emotions and think through a solution instead.

When your mom tells you to stop worrying about an argument you had with your friend, she is just trying to help you to react more logically to the situation.

45

Reflections

Have you ever kept a diary, a journal, or a blog? A nice way to remember a certain time or place is to keep a record of where you go and what you do. But writing down how you feel about what you do gives you a window into your brain. How do you respond and react to what's happening around you?

We all need to reflect sometimes. Try to make it a regular thing in your life— keeping in touch with your feelings can be creative too.

Try keeping a daily journal for a week (or longer if you enjoy it). Each night before you go to bed, write down your feelings about the day. You can describe what you did, but make sure you reflect on how you felt about it.

As a teenager you may make lots of decisions from your amygdala. But by reflecting on your feelings, you're putting your cortex to work too. You may find after keeping a journal for a week, your cortex might be better able to jump in during decision-making times and help you come up with good solutions to your problems.

Dear Journal, I made some great new friends at school today ...

give it a rest

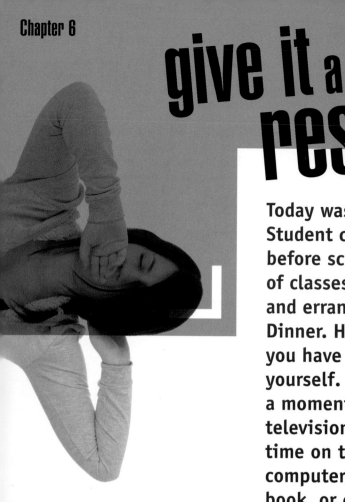

Today was just packed. Student council meeting before school. A full day of classes. Hockey practice and errands after school. Dinner. Homework. Finally you have a moment to yourself. Maybe you take a moment to watch television, spend time on the computer, read a book, or chat on the phone with your friends.

You should probably feel tired by now. It's 9:00 p.m. You have to wake up at 6:00 in the morning to even have a chance of catching the bus on time. But then it's 9:30 ... 10:00 ... 10:30 ... You're still not tired. Your parents are telling you to go to bed. But your body is telling you something different.

Natural Rhythm

Your body keeps a rhythm. Not because you're tap dancing or playing drums. Your body's circadian rhythm tells it when to wake and when to sleep. It is controlled by the hormone melatonin that's released by the brain. A hormone is a chemical, like a neurotransmitter, but instead of being released by a neuron, it is released by glands that send the chemical right into your bloodstream.

In teenagers, melatonin is released later in the evening. Even if you felt like falling asleep in your Spanish class earlier in the day, when it comes to time for bed, you may not actually be tired. Your circadian rhythm is set too late.

Rush, rush, rush! From practice to homework and meeting friends, you are always on the go. So why aren't you tired at bedtime?

Sleep Schedule

One of the best things for your body is a regular sleep schedule. That means going to bed around the same time each night and waking up around the same time too. Sleeping in on weekends can make up for some lost sleep, but if you *sleep* hours later than usual, your body gets confused. Try to keep your body in rhythm.

Keep a fixed bedtime and wakeup time for a week Monday through Friday.

Then on Saturday, when you don't have to wake up for school, see what happens. Did your body wake up on its own at the same time?

Enough Sleep?

Scientists say teenagers need about nine hours of sleep a night. Why? Sleep gives your whole body needed rest. Lack of sleep affects your ability to concentrate. It can make you feel down and unfocused. Your grades might suffer and you won't be able to play sports as well. When you're old enough to drive, you'll be putting yourself, your passengers, and other drivers at risk if you're sleepy behind the wheel.

The Sleep Cycle

Sleep works in cycles. There are five stages in a cycle—stage 1, stage 2, stage 3, stage 4, and REM sleep. During stages 1 and 2, your heart and breathing rates slow, but you can still be woken up easily. During stages 3 and 4, you sleep very deeply. Finally, REM sleep (REM stands for "rapid eye movement") is the stage when you dream. Each cycle lasts about 90 to 100 minutes. You go through four to six cycles a night.

Staying up late studying is not the best idea. It's better to study and then get a good night's sleep.

Still Active

Besides dreams, some scientists think your brain uses REM sleep to continue learning. In a study they watched the brain activity of a group of people learning a new task. During REM sleep they noticed the subjects' brains showed the same activity. They concluded that the brains were reviewing what they had learned during the day and firming up pathways to help them remember.

What does this mean for you? If you have a big test, you might think it makes sense to stay up all night studying. But you may actually do better if you study earlier and make time for a good night's sleep. Your brain can use this time to review the answers. You'll wake up ready to attack the test.

On Stage with Your Pants Down

Have you ever dreamed you have a big test in a class you've never attended? Or that you're the star of the school play, but you're completely naked? Dreams can be filled with monumentally embarrassing moments, terrifying monsters, impossible situations, and bizarre mixes of people and places from the day and memories from long ago.

Chemical changes occur in the brain when you're sleeping. The cortex goes "off line" and other parts explore your brain's memories.

Even if the situations in your dreams don't seem to make logical sense, you'll often find the emotions—such as happiness, fear, and panic—feel as real as when you're awake.

Sometimes that can help you work out problems. Maybe you're really frustrated with your language arts teacher for scheduling an oral report the same day as your basketball game. That night in a dream, you tell off your teacher enough to make him sob in despair. Even if you wouldn't dare stand up to him in real life, you might wake up feeling better the next morning. Your brain helped you vent those frustrations when you were asleep.

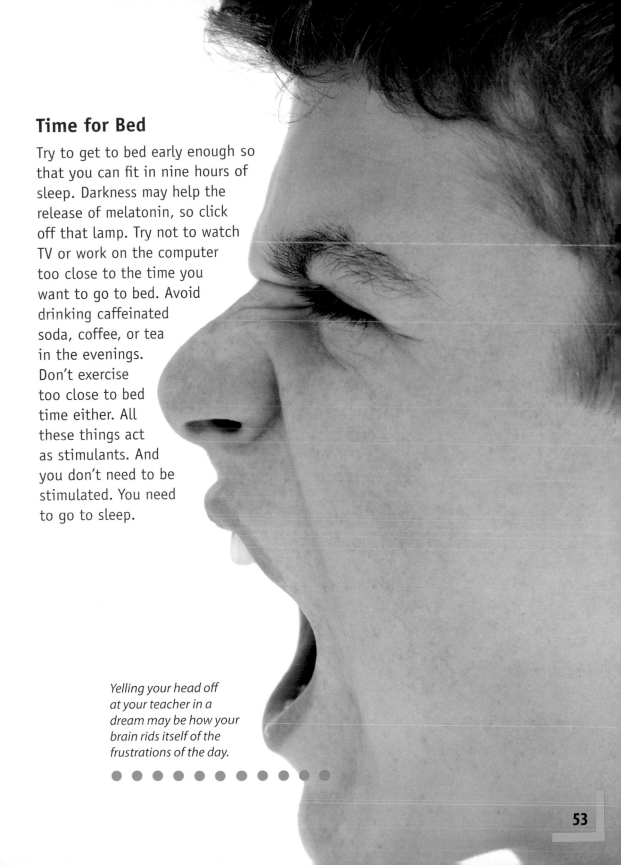

Time for Bed

Try to get to bed early enough so that you can fit in nine hours of sleep. Darkness may help the release of melatonin, so click off that lamp. Try not to watch TV or work on the computer too close to the time you want to go to bed. Avoid drinking caffeinated soda, coffee, or tea in the evenings. Don't exercise too close to bed time either. All these things act as stimulants. And you don't need to be stimulated. You need to go to sleep.

Yelling your head off at your teacher in a dream may be how your brain rids itself of the frustrations of the day.

defend the head!

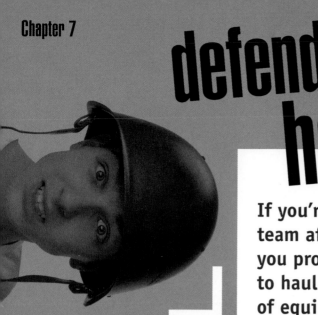

Shoulder pads—check!

If you're on a sports team after school, you probably have to haul around a lot of equipment—bats, balls, rackets, sticks. You also might have to wear protection—from shin guards to mouth guards, shoulder pads, and football helmets. These extra layers protect your body from a hard blow from a ball, an opponent, or the ground.

Your skull is like a helmet under your skin. Eight bones make up the top part that forms a protective shield around your brain. The meninges are three additional layers of tissue that surround the brain. There's also brain juice, called cerebrospinal fluid, floating around in your skull to protect your brain.

Helmet—check!

Mouth guard—check!

FACT!

Getting Inside

It's not easy for surgeons to access a brain. First they put the patient to sleep and cut into the scalp. Then they cut out a piece of the skull with a drill. This creates a fine bone dust. They open the skull to reach the area of the brain they need to work on.

At this point surgeons may need to wake up the patient. Since the brain itself does not have any pain nerves, surgeons can work on the brain while the patient is still conscious. As they work on certain parts of the brain, they can ask the patient specific questions to see if they are being successful.

Football players are taught how to tackle properly to protect against head and neck injuries.

Brain Damage

The cushions around your brain aren't always enough to protect it. Sometimes a fall or blow to the head makes the brain bang into the insides of the skull. Unlike breaking an arm or a leg, which can be reset and grow back into place, damage to your brain can't always be undone. Depending on where your brain is hurt, it might affect your ability to talk, move, feel, and think. It may be tempting not to wear a helmet when you're riding your bike, skiing or snowboarding, or skateboarding a half pipe. But damage to your brain could dramatically change your life or even kill you. One of your brain's main functions is to protect you. It's also worth it to protect your brain the best you can.

true tales

Blackout

When Katrina was on the sidelines at her lacrosse practice, a ball accidently hit her in the back of the head. "I didn't feel anything but numbness, then I blacked out," she says. Katrina felt disoriented. "I felt like I was hit by a bus and my vision was clouded by big black dots."

Katrina had a concussion. Concussions can make you feel dizzy, nauseous, and have trouble focusing. You may not be able to speak clearly. Even when you feel back to normal, your coach may not let you play for the rest of the game, or may make you wait even longer, to be sure you're OK.

Rules require male lacrosse players to wear helmets and pads to protect the head and upper body.

A football helmet has interior padding and an outer shell to protect a player's head.

Besides avoiding injuries, there are other ways you can take care of your brain. Foods such as fish, berries, broccoli, and even chocolate have been called brain foods for a reason. Protein makes you alert. Fats help your memory. Simple carbohydrates give you an energy boost, and complex carbohydrates help you feel full. Studies have shown that if you skip breakfast, you're more likely to feel unfocused in school. Never try to think on an empty stomach— your brain needs food.

Brain Exercises

You can exercise your brain by challenging it with puzzles and games. You can even exercise it with interesting conversations and debates. Every time you try something new, you give your brain more knowledge. When you play music, write a story, or sketch a picture, you're developing the creative parts of your brain. You even hone your brain skills when you do chores—painting a room, building a shed, or fixing a car. Everything you do stimulates your brain's power to make connections.

Your brain loves a fresh challenge. Learning something new can be tough, but trying a new skill helps your brain develop.

FACT!

Brain Farts

Do you ever make mistakes doing a really simple task? Some people call this a brain fart—a brief lapse in concentration that makes you mess up.

Scientists in Norway have studied brain farts. They had subjects perform a task over and over again while in an fMRI machine. They were surprised to see abnormal brain activity up to a half-minute before the subject made a mistake.

true tales

Protect and Survive

Snowboarder Shaun White was only 13 years old when he turned pro. And he was still just a teenager when he won a gold medal in men's snowboarding in the 2006 Olympics. Some snowboarders don't wear helmets because they think it looks lame. But White's not afraid to protect himself. He's made helmets look cool.

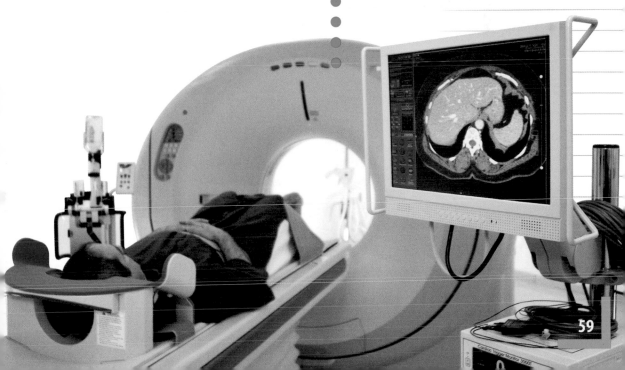

Imagine seeing your brain messing up! Scientists can see it on an MRI scanner.

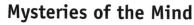

Mysteries of the Mind

With all the work your brain does, we still don't know the whole story. Scientists will be studying the human brain far into the future.

For now you have plenty of things to think about, such as protecting, feeding, and stimulating your growing brain. Your brain is busy making connections to last you a lifetime.

What is at the end of the universe? Stimulate your brain with big questions.

Outside the Box

Has anyone ever told you to think outside the box? In brain terms that means finding different pathways to come to a solution. Try this game to get your brain to find alternative ways to arrive at an answer.

You will need:
● List of tasks (right), or more that you make up on your own

Look at the list of tasks. The tasks themselves aren't hard to do, but you'll have to challenge yourself to do them in a new way.

1. Make a sandwich (without any bread).
2. Brush your teeth (with your hands behind your back).
3. Tell your friend about your day at school (without speaking).
4. Create a map (without paper or a pencil or pen).
5. Find page 56 of your textbook (with your eyes closed).

Were you able to think of a new, creative way to complete each task ? How hard was it for your brain to make new pathways to arrive at the result?

What's outside the box?!

glossary

amygdala—the emotional center of the brain

axon—a long fiber on a neuron that passes information along to the next cell

brain stem—the lowest part of the brain at the top of the spinal cord. It takes information from all parts of your body and helps you understand and sort through it.

cerebellum—the part of the brain that keeps you balanced

cerebrospinal fluid—a liquid in your skull that helps protect your brain

cerebrum—the main part of the brain that does most of the thinking

circadian rhythm—a daily cycle or pattern of activity

corpus callosum—a bridge of nerves that connects both hemispheres so they can communicate with each other

cortex—the outer layer of the cerebrum, also called gray matter

dendrites—the branches coming off one end of a neuron that take in information

hippocampus—the part of the brain that pulls separate information together to form a complete memory

hormone—a chemical released by glands into the bloodstream

hypothalamus—the part of the brain that links the nervous system with a system of glands, called the endocrine system

limbic system—the part of the brain that controls emotions and the release of chemicals in the body. It includes the hippocampus and the amygdala.

lobes—areas of the brain that serve various functions. There are four lobes on each hemisphere.

melatonin—a hormone that helps you maintain a cycle of sleeping and waking

meninges—layers of tissue surrounding the brain

neuron—a nerve cell

neurotransmitter—a chemical that transfers information between cells

phobia—an irrational fear

synaptic cleft—the space between neurons

additional resources

Read More

Bickerstaff, Linda. *Frequently Asked Questions about Concussions*. New York: Rosen Publishing Group, 2010.

Markle, Sandra. *Wounded Brains: True Survival Stories*. Minneapolis: Lerner Publications, 2011.

Newquist, H.P. *The Great Brain Book: An Inside Look at the Inside of Your Head*. New York: Scholastic Reference, 2004.

Stewart, Melissa. *You've Got Nerve! The Secrets of the Brain and Nerves*. New York: Marshall Cavendish Benchmark, 2010.

Internet Sites

Use FactHound to find Internet sites related to this book. All of the sites on FactHound have been researched by our staff.

Here's all you do:
Visit *www.facthound.com*
Type in this code:
9780756544867

index

About the author:
Dana Meachen Rau's brain is packed with information from researching more than 270 books for children, including titles about science, history, geography, biographies, early readers, and cookbooks. She does her thinking and writing in Burlington, Connecticut.